# Ralph Vaughan Williams
# Songs of Travel

To access companion recorded accompaniments online, visit:
www.halleonard.com/mylibrary

8008-6192-2904-7124

DISTRIBUTED BY

HAL•LEONARD®
CORPORATION
7777 W. BLUEMOUND RD. P.O. BOX 13819 MILWAUKEE, WI 53213

For all works contained herein:
Unauthorized copying, arranging, adapting,
recording, Internet posting, public performance,
or other distribution of the printed music in this publication is an infringement of copyright.
Infringers are liable under the law.

www.boosey.com
www.halleonard.com

# PREFACE

Ralph Vaughan Williams (1872–1958) composed art songs which are among the best British works in the genre, particularly in the first decade of the twentieth century. He composed a few art songs before 1900, but his earliest noteworthy song is "Linden Lea," composed in 1901. In the same year Vaughan Williams composed "Whither must I wander," which would become part of *Songs of Travel*. The remaining songs in the cycle, originally for baritone and piano, were composed in 1904. His 1903 song cycle *The House of Life*, which includes the perennial favorite "Silent Noon," is also from the same period. Other major works for voice from this early period in the composer's work are *A Sea Symphony* (composed 1903–09), and *On Wenlock Edge* (composed 1908–09). Vaughan Williams achieved wide and varied success in other genres, particularly with orchestral and choral pieces. He returned to song composition in the 1920s, producing 21 songs in that decade. The composer turned again to writing art songs in the 1950s. Vaughan Williams also made quite a few arrangements of English folksongs for voice and piano.

The first eight songs in *Songs of Travel* were first performed as a "complete" set in London in 1904. The ninth song, "I have trod the upward and downward slope" was discovered in the composer's manuscripts after his death by his widow, Ursula Vaughan Williams, and added in 1960 to the first complete edition of the cycle. The citation was added to the added song's publication: "This little epilogue to the Song Cycle *Songs of Travel* should be sung in public only when the whole cycle is performed."

The composer orchestrated "The Vagabond," "The Roadside Fire" and "Bright is the ring of words." British composer Roy Douglas, musical assistant to Vaughan Williams at one time, later orchestrated the remaining songs of the cycle, employing the same instrumentation used by Vaughan Williams.

The Scottish writer Robert Louis Stevenson (1850–94) is best remembered for his novels *Treasure Island*, *Kidnapped*, and the novella *The Strange Case of Dr. Jekyll and Mr. Hyde*. He enjoyed a celebrated reputation as an unconventional adventurer, and traveled widely in his short life in Europe and the United States before settling in Samoa. (He died there at a young age from a probable cerebral hemorrhage.) Stevenson was also a sometime composer and arranger, and set some of his poems to music himself. The poetry collection *Songs of Travel and Other Verses* was published posthumously in 1896. The following editor's note appeared in the original edition:

> The following collection of verses, written at various times and places, principally after the author's final departure from England in 1887, was sent home by him for publication some months before his death. He had tried them in several different orders and under several different titles, as "Songs and Notes of Travel," "Posthumous Poems," etc., and in the end left their naming and arrangement to the present editor...

There are 44 poems in Stevenson's *Songs of Travel and Other Verses*. From these Ralph Vaughan Williams chose nine. Stevenson's title for the poem used in the first song of the cycle is "The Vagabond (To an air of Schubert)." It is not known what Schubert song Stevenson had in mind. The song title "The Roadside Fire" is Vaughan Williams' (the poem appears without a title).

—Richard Walters

# PUBLISHER'S NOTE
# FROM THE 1969 HIGH VOICE EDITION

The Songs of Travel were not published in a complete edition until 1960, following the posthumous discovery of "I have trod the upward and the downward slope" (No. 9) amongst the composer's papers. The present complete edition (1969) for High Voice is published with the permission of Mrs. Ursula Vaughan Williams, and the publishers are also indebted for the assistance of Mr. Roy Douglas in its preparation. As in the Low Voice edition "Whither must I wander" (No. 7) has been transposed to fit in to the tonal sequence of the cycle as has, of course, No. 9; otherwise the high-voice transpositions remain the same as those originally published in two groups by Boosey & Co. in 1905 and 1907.

# CONTENTS

Pianist on the Recording: Laura Ward

The price of this publication includes access to companion recorded accompaniments online,
for download or streaming, using the unique code found on the title page.
Visit www.halleonard.com/mylibrary and enter the access code.

# The Vagabond

original key: a Major 3rd lower

ROBERT LOUIS STEVENSON

RALPH VAUGHAN WILLIAMS

**Allegro moderato**
*(alla marcia)*

*p ma sempre marcato*

*sempre pesante il basso*

Give to me the life I love, Let the lave go by me, Give the jol - ly heaven a - bove, And the by-way nigh me.

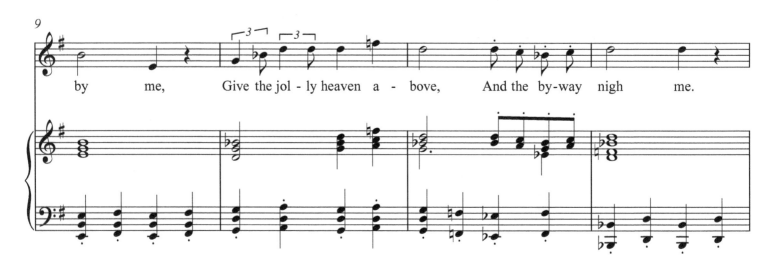

Bed in the bush with stars to see, Bread I dip in the ri-

ver— There's the life for a man like me,_____ There's the

life for ev - er.

Let the blow fall soon or late, Let what will be

o'er me; Give the face of earth a - round, And the road be - fore me.

Wealth I seek not, hope nor love, Nor a ___ friend to know

me; All I seek, the heaven a - bove, _____ And the

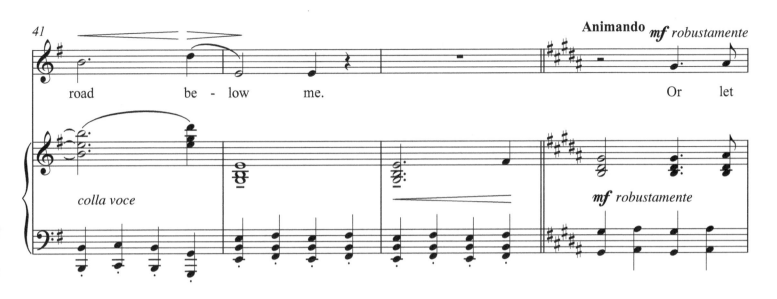

White as meal the fros-ty field— Warm the fire-side ha - ven—

Not to au-tumn will I yield, Not to win - ter

e - ven!

Let the blow fall soon or late, Let what will be o'er me; Give the face of earth a -

# Let Beauty awake

original key: a minor 3rd lower

ROBERT LOUIS STEVENSON

RALPH VAUGHAN WILLIAMS

cend, \_\_\_\_ Let her wake to the kiss of a ten - der friend, To

ren - der a - gain \_\_\_\_ and re - ceive!

# The Roadside Fire

original key: a Major 3rd lower

ROBERT LOUIS STEVENSON

RALPH VAUGHAN WILLIAMS

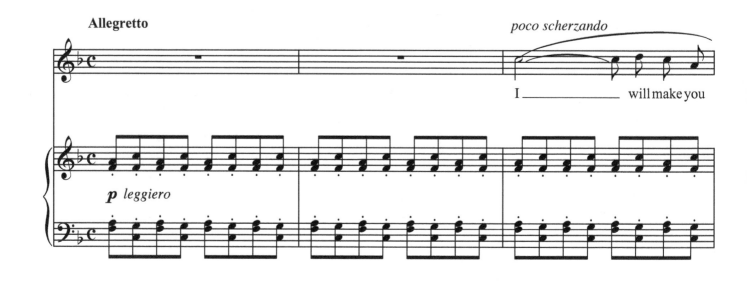

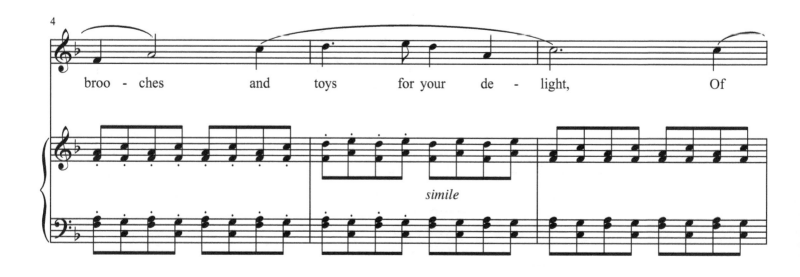

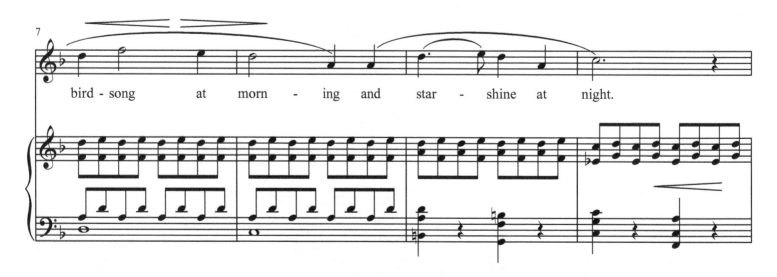

largamente

mem - ber, that on - ly you ad - mire, Of the

colla voce

pp

tranquillo

broad __ road that stretch - - -

pp

tranquillo

- - es and the road - - - side

fire. __

pp   pp una corda

8va

# Youth and Love

original key: a minor 3rd lower

ROBERT LOUIS STEVENSON

RALPH VAUGHAN WILLIAMS

Pass - ing ____ for ev - er, ____ he fares; ____ and on

ei - ther hand, Deep ____ in the gar - dens

gol-den pav - il - ions hide, Nes-tle in or - chard bloom, ____

poco f

p

pp

pp

# In dreams

original key: a minor 3rd lower

ROBERT LOUIS STEVENSON

RALPH VAUGHAN WILLIAMS

In dreams un - hap-py, I be - hold you stand as here - to-fore: The un - re-mem-ber'd to - kens in your hand a - vail no more. No more the morn - ing glow, no more the grace, en - shrines, en - dears.

# The infinite shining heavens

original key: a minor 3rd lower

ROBERT LOUIS STEVENSON

RALPH VAUGHAN WILLIAMS

The in-fi-nite shin-ing heavens Rose, __ and I saw __ __ in the night Un - count-a - ble an - gel stars Shower - - ing sor - row and light.

*In Stevenson's original poem this word is 'stood'.

# Whither must I wander?

original key: a minor 3rd lower

ROBERT LOUIS STEVENSON

RALPH VAUGHAN WILLIAMS

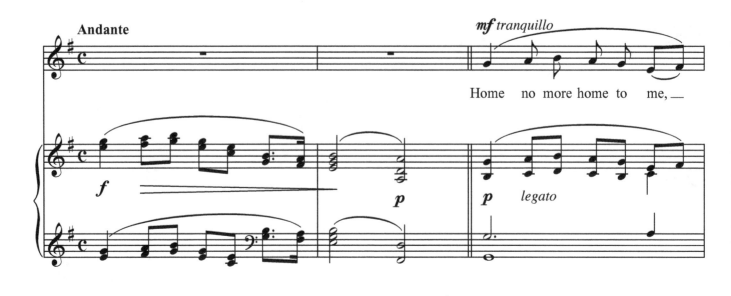

Home no more home to me, —

whi-ther must I wan - der? Hun-ger my dri - ver, I go — where I must.

Cold blows the win-ter wind — o-ver hill and hea - ther: Thick drives the

rain and my roof is in the dust. Lov'd of __ wise men was the shade of my roof-tree, The true word of wel-come was spo-ken in the door:— Dear days of old __ with the fa-ces in the fire - light; Kind folks of old, you __ come a - gain no more.

Home was home then, my dear, full of kind-ly fa - ces, Home was home then, my dear,_ hap - py for the child. Fire and the win-dows bright glit-tered on the moor - land; Song, tune - ful song, built a pa - lace in the wild. Now when day dawns on the brow _ of the moor - land, Lone stands the house and the

chim-ney-stone is cold. Lone let it stand now the friends are all de-part-ed, The kind hearts, the true hearts, that loved the place of old.

Spring shall come, come a-gain, call-ing up the moor-fowl, Spring shall bring the sun and rain, bring the bees and flow-ers; Red shall the hea-ther bloom o-ver hill and val-

# Bright is the ring of words

original key: a 4th lower

ROBERT LOUIS STEVENSON

RALPH VAUGHAN WILLIAMS

# I have trod the upward and the downward slope

original key: a 4th lower

ROBERT LOUIS STEVENSON

RALPH VAUGHAN WILLIAMS

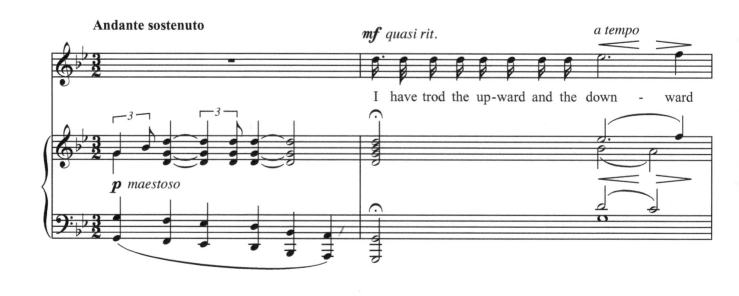

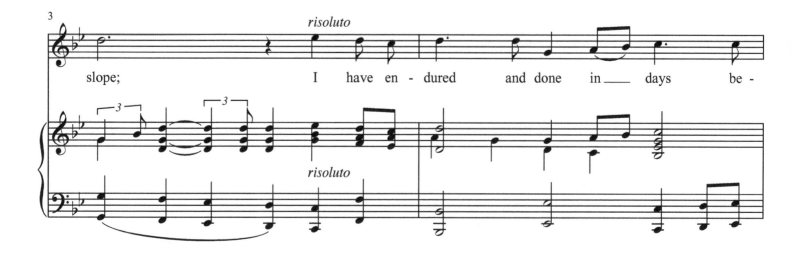

This little epilogue to the Song Cycle *Songs of Travel* should be sung in public only when the whole cycle is performed.

And I have lived and loved, and closed the door. ppp

door.